THE WHISPERING WILLOW TREE

VOLUME I POEMS
ANITA R. ESCHLER

Please note this is a work of fiction. Names, characters, incidents, and places are either a product of the author's imagination or are used fictitiously, and any resemblance to actual persons, living or dead, events, or locales is entirely coincidental.

The Whispering Willow Tree

Copyright © 2023 by Anita R. Eschler

All rights reserved.

Anita R. Eschler is to be identified as the author of these poems. No part of this publication may be reproduced, distributed, or transmitted in any form or by any means, including photocopying, recording, or other electronic or mechanical methods, without the prior written permission of the publisher, except in the case of brief quotations embodied in critical reviews and certain other non-commercial uses permitted by copyright law.

Scripture quotations marked (NLT) are taken from the Holy Bible, New Living Translation, copyright ©1996, 2004, 2015 by Tyndale House Foundation. Used by permission of Tyndale House Publishers, Carol Stream, Illinois 60188. All rights reserved.

Scripture taken from the New King James Version®. Copyright © 1982 by Thomas Nelson. Used by permission. All rights reserved.

Cover design/Formatting: Anita R.Eschler

Second Edition

Hardback ISBN 9780645076974

Table of Contents

Yours

The Frivolous Affair

Sacrifices

A Dogs Apothegm

Humanity

A Gift

Flickering Flecks

Dear Orphan, How You Mourn

Through the Tempest

Shifting Seasons

Magnificent Dream

Paradise

All For Your Glory

Captivate My Heart

Eternal Life

The Willow's Wisdom

Surrendered

Yours

I'm completely yours because you have my heart, life, and my soul;
This breath is yours, for you alone Lord, make me whole.

Your grace is unearned, undeserved, yet pours over me in abundance;
Thank you, Jesus, you suffered to free me from any encumbrance.

Your love flows like a river, rushing through the valleys of my heart;
A presence I cannot fathom not describe—where would I even start?

For you alone hold my paths in the palm of your hands;
For you alone are the rock on which I will stand.

"Be still and know I am God," You say;
So here I am on my knees—Lord, your command I will obey.

My arms lift to give you praise because I'm blinded by your brilliance;
For your mercy never fails, and your goodness shines with beaming radiance.

~Anita R. Eschler

"My old self has been crucified with Christ. [a] It is no longer I who live, but Christ lives in me. So I live in this earthly body by trusting in the Son of God, . who loved me and gave himself for me."
Galatians 2:20 (NLT)

The Frivolous Affair

A flurry of colourful feathers floated to the foliage below;
The flock of lorikeets taking flight—it was quite a vivid show.

They squabbled and squawked as they found the sweet nectar of a tree;
And proceeded to drink until intoxicated, no longer able to fly away free.

Raucous and rowdy, their volume increased as did their fun;
Hanging upside down and wrestling with each other in the glow of the late afternoon sun.

And across the road, humans mirrored their evening of parallel frivolity;
Only with less class and agility—and yet, with as much joviality.

~Anita R.Eschler

"Look at the birds of the air, for they neither sow nor reap nor gather into barns; yet your heavenly Father feeds them. Are you not of more value than they?"
Matthew 6:26 (NKJV)

Sacrifices

Sacrifices cause a ripple effect that reaches farther than you can perceive;
The subsequential lapping against the shore has more impact than you thought you could achieve.

Like the gradual erosion of sand to carry it across the vast tumultuous oceans;
One act of kindness will also reach, carrying on through each person and their motions.

A simple act of love, care and compassion is all that is needed for the resonated swell to take;
As simple as a leaf oscillating on a breeze before kissing the shimmering surface of the lake.

There are some married to the money, making more each day;
Too busy to appreciate the beauty around us—only focusing on the grey.

Missing simple pleasures like the sinking sun leaving a colourful palette in its wake,
Or the smell of fresh earth after rain, and a rainbow reflected across a lake.

They don't realise that each dawn delivers a beautiful new day, a new chance to live;
A new chance to love, and a new chance to give.

Cont.

It is far too easy to selfishly wallow in our own issues, but
perspective could open our murky eyes;
That there is always someone else out there who is worse off
and suffering—it is us up to us to open our hearing to their
cries.

Sacrifice was gifted to us, so we should gift it to others;
To anyone who needs it—to strangers, friends, to our sisters
and brothers.

~ *Anita R .Eschler*

"*She extends a helping hand to the poor
and opens her arms to the needy.*"
Proverbs 31:20 (NLT)

Child of His

Little child, you are loved and not alone;
This life is fleeting yet written in stone.

Lift your eyes toward a new tomorrow;
For there is One who will take your pain and sorrow.

Beyond the impossible is hope for more;
Just trust in Him for whatever He has in store.

Little child with wide haunted eyes and a dirt stained face;
Jesus will be your light, your everything—your saving grace.

~ Anita R .Eschler

But Jesus said, "Let the little children come to Me,
and do not forbid them; for of such is the kingdom of
heaven."
Matthew 19:14 (NKJV)

A Dogs Apothegm

There is much to learn from the life of a dog; their heart so full
of peace and loyalty,
Regardless of the harm inflicted upon them, they never hate,
only treating their masters as royalty.

Boundless amounts of love they gift and their lives simple
without yearning for more,
Only necessities needed to survive; just food, water and
affection—their lives are not a chore.

~ *Anita R. Eschler*

"The godly care for their animals,
but the wicked are always cruel."
Proverbs 12:10 (NLT)

Humanity

What is life without love as a purpose, without kindness as our goal,
When those suffer from our ignorance, so does our soul.

Too easy is it to lose sight of the importance of humanity,
With senseless possessions—with the significance of image—
blocking our sight and sanity.

We give too little, too late, before our ashes turn to dust in the dirt.
Life as we know it gone, only food for the worms, and our lack of generosity leaving a trail of hurt.

Lighter is our burden when relieved of earthly belongings, no longer weighing us down,
For when we die, we lose them anyway, so we might as well share them with suffering towns.

There is more room to love and give when we free our hearts of the chattels we hold dear;
So, relinquish any possessions and all the earthly things we fear.

~ Anita R. Eschler

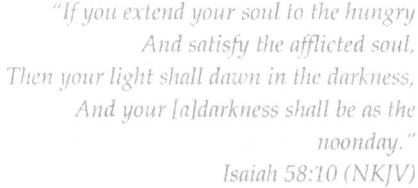

"If you extend your soul to the hungry
And satisfy the afflicted soul,
Then your light shall dawn in the darkness,
And your [a]darkness shall be as the noonday."
Isaiah 58:10 (NKJV)

A Gift

Pitter patter, scurry scatter, little feet scampering;
Wide eyes filled with wonder, a fire within not dampening.

Bright smiles, even through the vile, joyous beings with hints of heaven's gates;
Little hearts filled with love, regardless of the world's state.

Precious beings to be safeguarded — given a chance to bloom and grow;
Without the horrors of evil, or the corruption of humans diminishing their candle's glow.

A gift from God, a snippet of Himself, to treasure and nurture;
These little sparks of joy to light the world on fire, paving the way for a better future.

~ *Anita R. Eschler*

"Children are a gift from the Lord; they are a reward from him."
Psalm 127:3 (NLT)

Flickering Flecks

Do we lose our souls in the process of striving for the stars?
What does humanity even mean if we are no longer genuine,
our perceptions marred?

Could we possibly remain empathetic when our hearts are full
of materiality?
Or even when pretence is idolised to the point that we can no
longer discern reality.

Life is a flicker, a fleck, and our existence a speck on the
horizon of time;
Meaningless idols, conversations and goals occupy our
precious blimp on that chronological line.

Does what we do contribute at all, or is it as inconsequential as
gold leaf smattering a gourmet meal?
Necessity is no longer relevant—only the need for more
glamour to fill our empty soul, just so we can feel.

When all we need to survive is a bit of food and water, and
perhaps those we love to keep us warm;
It will be a day of reckoning for those relying on social status
when all that exists are plagues and swarms.

We reap what we sow, so how unfortunate for those who
traded their seeds,
All for the chance to be seen as someone other than who they
are; a lie and egotistical line of misdeeds.

Cont.

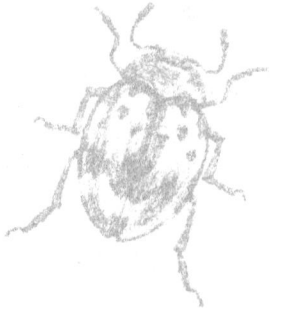

When does it all end? Well, some may think when we take our last breath,
Yet we forget our legacy and actions carry on, long after our insignificant death.

So, yes, it is important to live life to our fullest, though only if we remain pure in motive for all we do;
Otherwise, each day we lived is a waste—our hearts as blackened as the grime on the underside of our shoe.

Be kind, be better, be more than a photograph;
Give joy, give hope, and give genuine laughs.

Live life but with meaning—with purpose and with soul;
And fill that life with everlasting deeds, with love as your goal.

But live your life for the One who gave you breath;
Exalt and glorify God in all you do, until your death.

~ Anita R. Eschler

"Be still, and know that I am God;
I will be exalted among the nations,
I will be exalted in the earth!"
Psalm 46:10 (NKJV)

Dear Orphan, How You Mourn

The petite girl sat in her own filth, wide eyes overflowing with tears,
Pungent scents of decay and waste stung her nostrils, filling her with more fear.

Her swollen stomach was exposed, with tatted rags hanging from her malnourished frame,
Her childhood non-existent, with no joy or laughter, no place for a game.

Passer-by's ignored her cries, their own lives void of anything to offer,
Each villager in similar positions, each family in possession of an empty coffer.

Little did they know her only parent had died from their long journey to the river,
Her young Ma stolen while collecting dirty water — the men's intent to harvest her liver.

Perhaps they would decide they could fetch more if they sold her to a slaver,
Regardless, the mother would never see her toddler again; unless someone miraculously saved her.

The only hope for those in need come from the empathy and compassion of others,
We mustn't forget that we're all humans, even if not by blood — we're still all sisters and brothers.

Cont.

The smallest gift would create the largest ripple effect, even if that gift was one's time…
All it takes is a million people to open their hearts, even if only giving one dime.

We could finance those who could rescue the stolen — since their work would come at a price (as does everything worthwhile),
And yet, indirectly we would still be rescuing the stolen and giving those in need a reason to smile.

~ *Anita R. Eschler*

"Give justice to the poor and the orphan; uphold the rights of the oppressed and the destitute. Rescue the poor and helpless; deliver them from the grasp of evil people."
Psalm 82:3-4 (NLT)

Shifting Seasons

Seasons inevitably shift—from spring to summer, from the sun to the snow;
Just as our lives fluctuate, we cry and laugh, we live and grow.

The storms in our lives will pass, like the monsoons in the prairie;
Our moods will ebb like the tide and there are times we become weary.

Just remember during those times where we feel as if we're sinking;
That there is nothing we cannot face with some reflection and thinking.

Our trials will recede like the setting sun and ocean's shore line;
A new day will soon dawn and once more all in the world will be fine.

~Anita R. Eschler

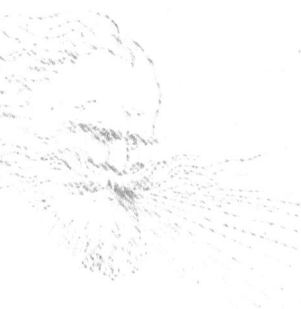

"To everything there is a season,
A time for every purpose under heaven."
Ecclesiastes 3:1
(NKJV)

Through the Tempest

The tempestuous storm raged, rolling through the hills,
Battering every tree, winds screaming forcefully and ever so shrill,

Little creatures hid in their shelters, trembling with fear,
Rabbits huddled close, snuggling with those they held dear,

But as quickly as the onyx cloud suffocated the blue sky,
The rain cleared up and in its place a rainbow, slowly passing by.

Trees were stronger from the assault, the grass and foliage flourished,
For through the turbulent storm, comes new life—all the living and dying are nourished.

~ Anita R. Eschler

*"Ask the Lord for rain in the spring,
for he makes the storm clouds.
And he will send showers of rain
so every field becomes a lush pasture."*
Zechariah 10:1 (NLT)

Magnificent Dream

The bubbling brook glimmered, gurgling as it leisurely ventured down,
Its surface like specks of diamonds sparkling on the face of a crown.

The sweet scent of nectar and dewy grass filled the air in its vicinity,
Alluring all manners of creatures drawn to the brook's divinity.

The deer knelt by its damp edge and graciously lapped at the fresh liquid,
Flinching at the first sip—the water very much frigid.

Needing hydration, it tentatively drank its fill,
Then elegantly rose on its legs and suddenly turned deathly still.

With twitching velvety ears and a flared nose, it intently listened,
Glancing around it looked, and its wide darting doe eyes glistened.

Upon hearing the rustling foliage farther upstream, it leapt into the woodland,
And a fierce tiger prowled into view, his banded coat magnificently grand.

The snakes slithered up the trees and little animals urgently scurried out of sight,
A kaleidoscope of colours burst as all the birds instantaneously took flight.

Cont.

With creatures loitering in the shadows, they watched in reverie from their hiding place,
Equally fearing and revering the king of the jungle and affording him some space.

The tiger's shiny coat shimmered at he ventured down to the stream,
When suddenly the scenery dissipated into a blur... I sat up in bed—the serene scene only my dream.

~ Anita R.Eschler

"For God may speak in one way, or in another,
Yet man does not perceive it. In a dream, in a vision of the night,
When deep sleep falls upon men,
While slumbering on their beds,
Then He opens the ears of men,
And seals their instruction."
Job 33:14-16 (NKJV)

Paradise

Gently undulating waves lapped against the pristine sandy shoreline,
Broken shells waltzed with the movement, tumbling against sand—both gritty and fine,

Seagulls sung as they circled above, their shadows made the crabs scuttle away,
The stretching band of beach was the bird's hunting ground—the bay providing adequate prey.

It was merely the circle of life; one little creature was another's sustenance,
Not aggressive in the least, just merely circumstance.

So as the habitat rotated self-sufficiently, the bay continued being nirvana,
Snakes sun-baked on the stones, just like the lizards; including the prickly iguana.

It closed its glistening eyes and tilted its thorned head to the sky,
Listening out for any meals to scurry past, for a tasty treat to flutter by.

Cont.

All wildlife was content, never wanting for more,
Even those old and dying, had never complained before.

For what a place to take one's last breath in, the best kind of serenity to sing one's last tune,
They all sang their own song, in their own way; they sang of their home in the dune.

~ Anita R. Eschler

"Yet God has made everything beautiful for its own time. He has planted eternity in the human heart, but even so, people cannot see the whole scope of God's work from beginning to end."
Ecclesiastes 3:11 (NLT)

All For Your Glory

Forgive me dear Father for my trangressions and mistakes;
I lay my life and soul at Your feet—I know what's at stake.

I'm your vessel and You're my anchor, please keep me in moor;
Fill me with more compassion and kindness so I can extend love to the poor.

Let everything I do, be for Your glory and honour—without any greed;
Help me be others nourishment, planting joyfulness as a seed.

Thank you for my blessed life, for shelter, food, water and those who hold me dear;
Thank you for healing my heart each time it breaks and I shed a tear.

I'm yours and you are mine.

~Anita R.Eschler

"If we confess our sins, He is faithful and just to forgive us our sins and to cleanse us from all unrighteousness."
1 John 1:9 (NKJV)

Captivate My Heart

Your every breath is an echo upon my heart;
Every inhale is a tattooed arrow and every exhale a dart.

Each kiss is like a flock of birds launching into the air to take flight;
taking me higher with each flap, yet never leaving sight.

Every sigh sings to me, a song floating on whisper—forever engrained in my memory;
The existence of your love breathes life into me, palpating externally.

It brings the sun out of dawn, littering the sky with pastel pinks and blue;
Painting my soul as forever yours and captivating my heart with every 'I love you'.

~ *Anita R.Eschler*

"Kiss me and kiss me again, for your love is sweeter than wine."
Song of Solomon 1:2 (NLT)

Eternal Life

Possessions matter not in this world for moths and corrosion
will eventually destroy their worth;
Money has no value in death, only floating upon the wind —
lost when their owners are buried deeply within the earth.

Bones and flesh are gnawed on by beasts then slowly eaten by
worms until evidence of existence has perished;
Status crumbles, like the dilapidated buildings that once
flourished — like a being's prized belongings that were once
cherished.

Invisible monsters ravish the earth, their forms disguised as
greed and vanity — the vanquishers of this civilisation;
Humans fall for their alluring deceit and glamour, the nature of
us causing the downfall of each nation.

We are our own demons, causing the grief of others — our
egotism disregarding the poor;
We do not deserve mercy, for it is the innocents of this world
neglected of their need — it is them we choose to ignore.

Life is but a fragile zephyr — gone with an instant, yet
worthwhile on a scorching day, a valuable contribution;
Each breath is a waste of oxygen — air that could be
implemented, unless helping those in destitution.

Cont.

So those reading this message, you are provided with the
knowledge of the utmost importance;
That this earth is in despair and in great need of kindness—in
need of less greed and riddance of malicious influence.

Otherwise, the downfall of humanity will be imminent, and
love will no longer bloom;
Evil will prevail our species—vanquishing kindness until all
that remains is doom.

~ Anita R. Eschler

"Do not lay up for yourselves treasures on earth, where
moth and rust destroy and where thieves break in and steal;
but lay up for yourselves treasures in heaven, where neither
moth nor rust destroys and where thieves do not break in
and steal. For where your treasure is, there your heart will
be also."
Matthew 6:19-21 (NKJV)

The Willow's Wisdom

A willow's wisdom lies in its roots, giving life for countless years,
Weeping for the dying woodland's creature's—its sap leaking a thousand tears.

The whispering willow wavers in the wind, wanting for nothing, only water and sun.
Just as flowers blossom in perfect timing; never rushed, otherwise becoming undone.

Mountains rarely move, content where they stand,
Merely mammoth statues, yet serene, and peacefully grand.

Simplicity surrounds us yet somehow evades our lives;
We notice too late, withering away with meaningless idols that become our wives.

Married to the money, making more each day,
Too busy to appreciate the beauty around us, only focusing on the grey.

The sun dips down below the diameter, dying another death,
Yet death brings life and rejuvenation; it births another breath.

Dawn delivers a new day, a new chance to live.
A new chance to love, and a new chance to give.

~ Anita R.Eschler

"Just ask the animals, and they will teach you. Ask the birds of the sky, and they will tell you. Speak to the earth, and it will instruct you. Let the fish in the sea speak to you. For they all know that my disaster[a] has come from the hand of the Lord. For the life of every living thing is in his hand, and the breath of every human being."
Job 12:7-10 (NLT)

Surrendered

My Life is not my own

These blessings are Yours you've sown

These hands are Yours to move

With only one motive and nothing to prove

These feet Yours to lead

Let my life be Your light, a seed

Because this heart belongs to You

And I glorify Your name in all I do

These eyes are only fixed upon You

My face turned toward heaven too

Wherever You need me, I am there

My time, love, and finance are Yours I'll share

Whenever You open doors, I'll be ready

Because even amongst the storm You keep me steady

This tarnished soul is Yours, and Yours alone

For You love me unconditionally to the depths of my bones

I am Your vessel to move.

I am Your lips to speak.

I am here to serve.

Only You.

Always You.

~ Anita R. Eschler

"...present your bodies a living sacrifice, holy, acceptable to God, which is your [b]reasonable service. And do not be conformed to this world, but be transformed by the renewing of your mind, that you may prove what is that good and acceptable and perfect will of God.
Romans 12:1-2 (NKJV)

Accolades

Above all, I thank my heavenly Father. God has given me all I need and more. I praise Him with every breath I take, until I take my last.

Jesus, let everything I do glorify You, let my light shine to magnify Your name.

I surrender.

I am yours.

~ Anita

www.ingramcontent.com/pod-product-compliance
Lightning Source LLC
Chambersburg PA
CBHW011352160426
42811CB00098B/1009